The Mind of a Grasshopper

INSPIRED POETRY BY

ANNIE L. VARNER

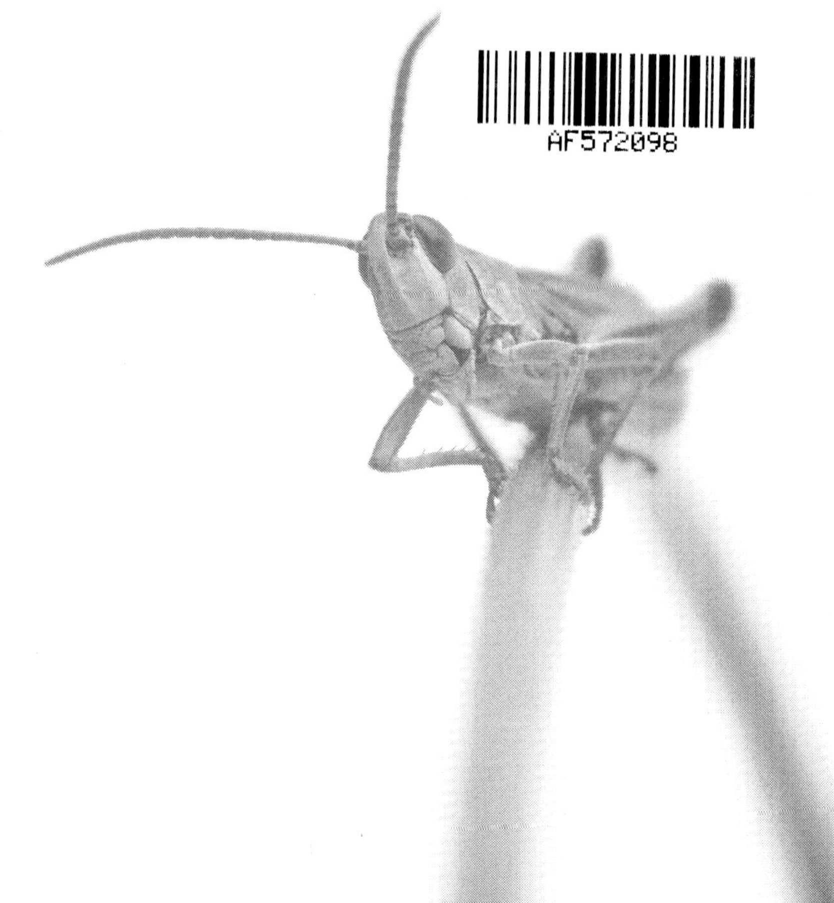

The Mind of a Grasshopper

INSPIRED POETRY BY

ANNIE L. VARNER

HUNTER ENTERTAINMENT NETWORK

Colorado Springs, Colorado

The Mind of a Grasshopper, Inspired Poetry by Annie L. Varner

First Edition: September 2017

To order products, or for any other correspondence:

Hunter Entertainment Network
4164 Austin Bluffs Parkway, Suite 214
Colorado Springs, Colorado 80918
Tel. (253) 906-2160 – Fax: (253) 912-1667
E-mail: contact@hunter-ent-net.com
Or reach us on the internet: www.hunter-ent-net.com

"Offering God's Heart to a Dying World"

This book and all other Hunter Entertainment Network™, Hunter Heart Kids™, and Hunter Heart Publishing™ books are available at Christian bookstores and distributors worldwide.

Chief Editor: Gord Dormer
Cover design by Phil Coles Independent Design
Logos & Layout Design: Exousia Marketing Group

ISBN: 978-1-937741-20-4
For Worldwide Distribution, Printed in the United States of America.

The Word of God says that as a man thinking in his heart, so is he. So, what are your thoughts on your vision, dreams and gifts? As you focus on the vision, where is it going? As you focus on the dreams, how will you achieve them? As you focus on your gifts, how will you relay them to the world? This book is for the gifted, the visionaries & the dreamers!

Acknowledgements

I want to take a moment to thank my children. My desire for them is to always be blessed and to achieve all that God has for them to do on this side. Samuel and Einna, may you always walk with God, for He is the Helper and Giver of life.

Many thanks to my family whom God has given to me. I appreciate all of you for believing in me, as I choose to go about serving God.

- **P**our out your soul to the world.
- **O**pening the door to new ideas, hopes, dreams, vision, thoughts & horizons.
- **E**ver increasing in wisdom and knowledge and understanding.
- **T**here is value in all these things.
- **R**unning in this race of life.
- **Y**ielding to the new you!

Table of Contents

Introduction

And the Lord spoke unto Moses saying, "Send thou men, that they may search the land of Canaan, which I give unto the children of Israel: of every tribe of their fathers shall ye send a man, everyone a ruler among them." (Numbers 13: 1-2, King James Version)

And Caleb stilled the people before Moses, and said, let us go up at once, and possess it. And there we saw the giants, the sons of Anak, which come of the giants: and we were in our own sight as grasshoppers, and so we were in their sight. (Numbers 13: 30 & 33)

Man took it upon himself, to say of himself that we were in our own sight as grasshoppers. Therefore, man predicted, or prophesied, his own state of being. It was not what God said. Mankind continues to see himself less than what God says about him, to this day.

Two of the men returned to Moses with a positive report, because they believed they were well able to possess the land. However, the other men gave an evil report saying, "They will crush us. They are giants and we look like grasshoppers beside them."

God's Word does not call His children grasshoppers, for that is the name given to a grasshopper. God's Word does say that as a man think in his heart so is he. In Philippians 4:8, it states: "Finally brethren, whatsoever things are true, whatever things are honest, whatsoever things are just, whatsoever things are of a good report if there be any virtue, and if there be any praise, think on these things."

Let your thoughts be in agreement with the Word of God. Let His Word rule in your heart. Conquer, rather than being conquered. Overcome, rather than being taken. How they saw themselves is how they believed and perceived themselves to be. Stop seeing yourself as something you do not want to be.

Note from the Author

These poems are a reflection of how I see within, whenever I think of what the Creator has said in His Word, regardless of how I feel. For faith in God is not a feeling, but an acceptance of the truth. "As a man thinks in his heart, so is he."

~Annie

Poetry Inspired by

Annie L. Varner

First Things First

Sitting in the morning sun
Was the grasshopper having fun.
He had stopped many on the way
To hear what Jesus had to say.

Psalms 100:4

"Enter into his gates with thanksgiving and into his courts with praise, be thankful unto Him and bless His name."

You see Mr. Grasshopper; your first ministry is to God
By praising Him and thanking Him.
Then, the Lord will do His part
To make Jesus the center of man's heart.
Truly it is not hard, just think on the air you breathe
It was God who made it possible.
The food you eat, it was God who made it possible.
The water you drink, it was God who made it possible.
So, thanksgiving and praise are the first words on your lips.
Daily, as we acknowledge WHO God is in our lives.
God made it possible.

Annie L. Varner

The Earth

The earth was without form
And void, until the voice of God was heard.
He brought light into the dark.
He created man in His image.
He set the law of the Land into His hand.
Adam failed the test and got us all in a mess.
He tried his way, but it didn't pay
So heaven was lost that very day.
Now man was sent from the Garden of Light
Unto a land where he must fight
The enemy with his might.
Man lost a life of ease
To pay for his misdeed.

Deceived

Hi Mr. Grasshopper, have I got news today
It's about a woman who lost her way.
That woman was deceived so
God's plan for woman
Started with Eve
As the story progressed
She got in a mess
She was deceived
By the serpent and his misdeeds.
To Adam was given the woman
To share in the beauty of Creation
For God saw that it was good
They were to be as one
But God's decision was not done.

Genesis: 3:2-3(KJV)

"And the woman said unto the serpent, we may eat of the fruit of the trees of the garden. But of the fruit of the tree which is in the midst of the garden, God hath, said "You shall not eat of it neither shall you touch it, least you die."

Spiritual death came into play and heaven was lost that very day
everything that's pleasing to the eyes can sometimes turn out to be a lie.
Deception played a major role and got Eve to lose control
Eve was disobedient and did not listen to the words of the Lord.
Adam shared with her sin, now they both were in a mess
Adam should have taken a stand and rebuked Eve's entire plan
God had placed all in his hand, but he shared with her mistake
And took the fruit and also ate.

Annie L. Varner

What Do You See?

As I walked alone the dusty road
The beauty of nature began to unfold
I saw the sun shining bright and pictured the stars at night.
I saw the trees and its shapes and forms to hide us in the midst of storms
I saw the animals running free and thoughts of Jesus came to me
Because His life and death and resurrection set me free
Reconciling man to God's original plan
Then, as my eyes turned toward the fence
I saw the grasshopper looking at me.
My thoughts went back in years and thoughts of Moses appeared
He leads the people to the land
Now it was time for them to stand
But many saw themselves as grasshoppers in the giant's land
Nevertheless, God's Word said to possess the land
And that is where man must stand.
As the wind blew across my face
I thought now of the human race.
Jesus appeared in my mind
True life can I find
I know I must renew my mind
And get in the process with time.

The Giants

When the Lord said, "Go, spy out the land."
The enemy's plot was to steal from man.
The spies went ahead and returned with the
Message and they were scared.
To them, they seemed like grasshoppers in their sight.
The land of the giants and their might
The Lord said spy out the land
Arise man and take a stand
God's Word stands true
Telling you what to do.
For victory is on His mind as we move in His time
The giants came in the land to take the power from man
But God had another plan and it was to possess the land
Now when the Lord says "Go", let us go
Now when the Lord says "Sit", let us sit
Let us wait patiently and do not quit.

Annie L. Varner

The Grasshopper and I

Numbers 13:33

I met the grasshopper on the way
He said you better keep your feet, so you don't stray
Keep your mind because I'm right on time, being deceitful in every way
The grasshopper revealed to me how he wants me to be
Cast down sicknesses all around, poor, hungry, lustful, envious, hateful, evil and always in strife, the package plan available to man.
So I said to the grasshopper, "I'm going to tell you how man should be."
Now first of all, there was a great fall
But the Master said, "I'll redeem them all!"
Why, they are the image and likeness of Me and I'm going to set them free.
By the shedding of blood man will see what man means to Me
By His name and through His name shall all of the world be claimed
Now grasshopper, listen to this. Open your ears, so you can't miss
Greater is He in me than He that is in the world
Do you know what that means; well it means that God and I are a team
I don't have to waiver to-and-fro
For His Word contains power, I know
So grasshopper, if God says possess the land
I'll stand firm on His command
For He is the beginning and the end
He knows your enemies, as well as your friends
And the only way with God is to win.

Finding Truth

Grasshopper, you lied from the beginning
Now the course must be set for
Man in winning
We have to accept the changing of the times and renew our minds.
If man wants to find truth
He must be true.
For what man sows
That also will he reap.
If man wants the promise from above
He can find it in God's love
1 Corinthians 13
If man wants to find God
He must allow God in his heart
Not forsaking his part.
God's love is peace.
God's love is joy.
God's love is righteousness.
Grasshopper, the choice for man is to find truth in this land.
By studying God's Word and taking a stand.

The Plan

The Lord established a plan for man
But man wanted to do things his way
Only man's way doesn't pay
Look closely at the Word of God
And let it captivate your heart; meditate on it and do your part
In **Proverbs 3:5**,
"Trust in the lord with all thine heart, and lean not unto thine
own understanding"
So a lie was placed in front of Eve's face and that's how man
fell from grace.
Lies lead away from God and the heart become dark
Lies are ticks of the enemy, like quicksand, taking away God's plan
Quicksand, taking over the life of man
Quicksand... quicksand... pulling you deeper out of God's reach
So God took a firm stand for salvation to redeem man with
His plan.

Reality

Walking along the dusty road
My thoughts began to unfold.
I saw God in the midst of it all.
In the beginning was the Tree of Life
In the Garden it all began
The existence of man and where he was to stand.
So much happened in that place
It took over the human race
Man was given dominion over the work of God's hand.
In a matter of time, man made a mess
Then, his future life was put to a test
Once he turned to the other side, all his beauty and grace just died.
Before the beginning of time
Man was on God's mind
He gave man an image and form.
Then, man was made whole
And became a living soul
Now to return to our rightful place.

The Creator's Way

Oh Grasshopper, don't you know
The way to God is not for show
Look to Jesus for He was meek and lowly of heart
From sin He wanted us to part.
Now listen to this and open your ears so you can't miss
The point you see is what Jesus did for the human race
In order to gain our rightful place
The plan was held by God's grace.
By that grace, we got to know the Creator's ways
Adam lost the way, but Jesus' plan will stay
Now each man must take his stand to discover God's plan.
How do you fit in His plan for your life?
How to live every day the Christ like way?
How to live the abundant life? How to walk with God?
Did you know grasshopper in **Genesis 5:24**
That Enoch walked with God; and he was not, for God took Him?
Now, you old grasshopper have been caught in the mist of your plan
But God stepped in and said, "I will deliver man."

The Battle Ground

In the midst of despair
I could see the grasshopper there
I saw man in the face of God who cared
True life man will never find
Until Jesus Christ became the center of his mind.
I knew in a moment of time
The grasshopper would display his mind
To try and find if he had found another foolish man
To trick and steal from God's hand.
Man's mind is the battle ground for the soul.
Don't lose it and get out of control
For it is the part that makes man hold.
If the grasshopper takes your soul away
You will not make it from day to day.
Don't give in for then he will surely win
Think on things that are pure
And they will lead to being sure
Don't give him any time with thoughts
Of doubt in your mind.
Let peace rule in your mind and in your heart, then you will have
done your part.

Despair

In the midst of despair, I could see the grasshopper sitting there
I saw man in the face of God who cared.
True life man will never find unless Jesus Christ became the
center of his mind
I knew in a moment of time the grasshopper would display his mind.
Man's mind is the battle ground for the soul
It is the part that makes man whole.
If the grasshopper takes it away, he will be destroyed day by day.
Man don't faint, or give up, but hold onto God's unchanging hand,
look beyond what you see
FOR JESUS DIED FOR YOU AND ME, SO WE COULD LIVE
IN VICTORY!
The grasshopper seemed to be asleep
As Jesus' words just put him to defeat
Depression and despair, take your turns and float on in the air.

Build Your Ark of Faith

Oh grasshopper, time is out for listening to you
I must move in the light of truth.
Now grab a hold of this
To please God is not a myth.
Noah held faith in his hand
And went about the Master Plan as a man.
Obedience came into play and that was going to show him the way
Build and pray for it will rain one day.
He didn't waiver to-and-fro for he knew faith was the way to go.
You see, faith is the substance of things hoped for
The evidence of things not seen.
Noah knew what all that means, so regardless to what the
people were saying
He took the words of God to heart and did his part
Not questioning what had to be done
So Noah and his family were kept from harm.
Noah had what it took
A willing mind and a heart for God
A desire to be a winner doing his part.
A listening ear discerning self and taking the test
And helping others save themselves.

Assignment

Grasshopper, let us make this clear to you.
John 1:14
"And the Word was made flesh and dwelt among us, and we beheld
His glory, the glory
Of the only begotten of the Father full of grace and truth."
He was made flesh and came to dwell among us.
Jesus had an assignment from Father God and had to do his part
Jesus was born into this world to bring the message from above.
When you get that straight
Your life will not be in the hands of fate.
Jesus became man to prove the Master Plan
His plan was to show man God is working on that plan.
Now arise, and take your stand
Helping as you can.
With Christ in you, the hope of Glory
That supernatural power from above
To help man rule in this world.

No Way

The grasshopper met me on the way and said, "Stop, let us play."
I turned and looked into his eyes and said, "NO WAY!"
I then said could we just sing and pray
The grasshopper said, "NO WAY! Who wants to pray?"
I said listen Jesus is the center of my heart
The grasshopper said, NO WAY! That is not my role!"
But I want to be in control of the children of God
That will keep them from doing their part
As I confuse their heart.
To be in control I must have their soul
Then I said, "NO WAY!"

The Lord is the Master of my soul.
And only He can be in control.
Each day I receive His grace and
Take my place in the human race
Knowing one day we will meet face to face.
As the grasshopper said, "NO WAY," I just ignored
What he had to say.

New

Mr. Grasshopper, what's new today? I guess you thought you could have your way
Let's look at what Jesus had to say.
Looking at the Book of Life, I came upon some startling advice
Jesus was the plan of God to work with men and convert the heart.

John 3:5

"Except a man be born of water and the Spirit, he cannot enter into the Kingdom of God"
Now read that slow and the truth of God will show.
One day as John stood baptizing in the river Jordan, he looked and saw Jesus coming and said, "Behold the Lamb of God!"
Jesus was then baptized and we must accept the fact of the new birth
Go down, get up, and renew the mind and true life you'll find
Salvation is meant for all mankind, as you renew your mind.

Being Baptized

The Grasshopper stood by the sea
Looking, staring at man, not regarding the MASTER plan
All about Redemption for man
He was thinking up another plan to trick man.
Why should they be baptized?
As I looked at him, thoughts of Eve came to me
Not again would the grasshopper win
When I looked again, I saw Jesus, our example to follow
He walked right into the water to be baptized
He went down and came up with resurrection power!
That was part of the plan right from God's hand
A part of the spiritual process for man
Man doing his part from his heart
Jesus makes it very clear in **John: 3: 5 (KJV)**
"Verily, Verily, I say unto thee, Except a man be born of water and of the Spirit, he cannot enter into the kingdom of God." That which is born of the flesh is flesh: and
That which is born of Spirit is spirit."

New Birth

Listen grasshopper, you don't know what to say
Clouds of confusion start your day
I pity the fool who thinks you are cool.
I know for a fact
The words of the Lord are exact
You can say this or you can say that
But the ALMIGHTY is where it's at!
He said in order to enter into His Kingdom
You must know His Son and only then you get the work done.

Roman 10:9 (KJV)

"That if thou shalt confess with thy mouth the Lord Jesus and shalt believe in thine heart that God hath raised him from the dead thou shalt be saved."

Man must get that in his heart
That is the beginning of his part.
Then look at **John 3:5**
That is what Jesus said to do
Go down, get up, and renew the mind
Start with God's time.

New Creature

Attention, attention Mr. Grasshopper
Have I got something to tear you apart
And it all comes from my heart.
Reading the Word, the other day
God showed me a new way.
Now listen to this. Open your ears, so you can't miss
God's way is plain
2 Corinthians 5:17
"Therefore if any man be in Christ, he is a new creature:
Old things are passed away; behold, all things are become new."
That means I can become a new creature in Christ
The words of the Lord can't be understood by a carnal heart.
You have got to turn your thoughts around
And then the Lord can be found.
Mr. Grasshopper, do you get it now?
If any man be in Christ, he is a new creature. New! New!
Change your thoughts, change your way, change your heart for a new day. Change by reading:
Philippians 4:8
"Finally, brethren, whatsoever things are true, whatsoever things are honest, whatsoever things are just, whatsoever things are pure, whatsoever things are lovely, whatsoever things are of a good report, if there by any virtue, and if there be praise, think on these things."

Not Only Bread

Oh grasshopper you are old
And set in your ways.
But Jesus has the last say.
Remember when He told you
Man shall not live by bread alone
But every word that precedes out of the mouth of God.
Matthew 4:4 states that and it is a living fact
So you see, each man must do his part and serve a living God
Not only that physical bread, but the spiritual Bread of Life
Was written for you and me
In Psalms 23 (KJV)
"Thou prepare a table before me in the presence of mine enemies, my cup runneth over."
Psalm 23 is personal to me
He is also anointing my head with oil
That fresh anointing, I need each day for the Lord is my Shepherd and will lead the way
And my cup runneth over with goodness and mercy also following me all of the days of my life,
And I will dwell in the house of the Lord forever.
So, the bread I eat is learning at Jesus' feet.

It is Written

Grasshopper, it is written for us today
To abide by what the Bible says.
I lift up my hands and begin to pray
In Jesus' name, God help me not to stray.
May goodness and mercy stay close by me
For I trust in the Lord with all my heart and from sin depart.
I delight myself in what God has done and commit to what He says
I rest in Him to bring things to pass knowing His promises will last
His Word is my wand and as I confess what God says about me it brings me total victory!

Proverb 30:5 (KJV)

"Every word of God is pure; He is a shield unto them that put their trust in Him."

Psalm 4:8

"I will both lay me down in peace, and sleep: for Thou, Lord, only makest me dwell in safety."

Ecclesiastes 3:1

"To ever thing there is a season, and a time to every purpose under the sun."

Roman 2:10

"But glory, honor, and peace, to every man that worketh good, to the Jew first, and also to the Gentile."

Ecclesiastes 12:13

"Let us hear the conclusion of the whole matter: Fear God and keep His commandments for this is the whole duty of man."

His Armour

So now Mr. Grasshopper
Put a lid on your mouth
For out of it comes the work of your heart.
You are filled with weakness
You are a great deceiver
You are a pain for all believers.
You lie, cheat, rob, and steal
Your ways are not real.
It's time now to turn the people around
And get all Christians heaven bound.
We are going to put on the whole armour of God and out of your reach we will depart.
These are the words that Jesus said
We are going to put them on and move ahead
Not acting like we're crushed and dead
So hold on tight, get this inside with all your might.

In Ephesians 6:13-17(KJV)

"Wherefore take unto you the whole armour of God,
That you may be able to withstand in the evil day, and having done all, to stand
Stand therefore, having your loins girded about with truth, and
Having on the breastplate of righteousness;
And your feet shod with the preparation of the gospel of peace;
Above all, taking the shield of faith, wherewith ye shall be able to quench all of the fiery darts of the wicked.
And take the Helmet of salvation, and
The sword of Spirit, which is the Word of God;

The Mind of a Grasshopper

Praying always with all prayer and supplication in the Spirit and
watching there unto with all perseverance and supplication
for all saints."
Begin to look into the mirror of your mind for Jesus is right on time.
He has a lot to say, so pay attention to the way.
The Bible is your message from God, now man must do his part
You've got to study to win
You've got to be ready my friends
Each day you start a new by asking Jesus what to do.
His way is His Father's Word
Set aside some time and pray
So God can make you ruler of the day
For we war not against flesh and blood
But the invisible realm of darkness
Take your feet and begin to stand, putting
On the amour given to man
Stopping Satan and his plan.

Keys to the Kingdom

Good morning grasshopper
Today it is time to shine
For Jesus has captured my mind.
Matthew 16:19
"And I will give unto you the keys of the kingdom of heaven:
And whatsoever thou shalt bind on earth,
Shall be bound in heaven.
And whatsoever thou shalt loose on
earth, shall be loose in heaven."
You know grasshopper
Jesus is the door keeper
The keys can only be used if you know Him.
Jesus made it very clear
That He would build His Church and the gates of hell shall not
prevail against it
So, man must not fear just open his ears so he can hear
The truth of the matter is God made a way for man to return
back to Him.

Partnership

Grasshopper, how is it going today?
I've got a message, so you have to stay.
Listen to the facts and just hold on to your hat. It's about partnership with God coming out of a pure, wholesome clean heart that trusts in a living God.
A husband and wife team coming together, facing life and what it means
The trust of partnership comes from within to bring us together as lovers and friends
The blueprint of faith and it all started on our first date.
Each must work from their heart and do their rightful part.
Partnership works through many tests, so bury the past and start afresh.
Looking ahead for what to do, begin to renew your mind, a true relationship will come in time.
You old grasshopper had a partnership with God, but you let envy overtake your heart
And wanting to take away from God
Knowing God gave you your part.
So, as we see what happened to you
Our relationship with God must be true, seek Him first, humble yourself and He will
Tell you what to do
A partnership that's true.

The Way

Grasshopper, don't you know
The way to God is not a show.
Look to Jesus, He was meek
And humble of heart
He was the Son of God doing His part.
His mind was set for the Master's plans
To be met.
Your mind must be renewed to focus on God's views
Now listen to this and open your ears
Grasshopper, you wanted control for years
But the point, you see, is what Jesus did
Through His sweat and tears
So that man may regain all the years.
Adam had a relationship with God
God created a Garden and put him in charge
God gave him authority to be part of Him
God and Adam were a friendly pair.
Our hearts must be true
We'll have to seek the heart of God
Look within and do our part
In **Ephesians 1:14**
"According as he hath chosen us in Him before
The foundation of the world that we be holy and without blame."
Before Him in love with that in mind
You must begin to work with time.

In Time

Before the beginning of time, man was on God's mind.
He took His thoughts within to create a man to be His friend.
After pondering the way, God created man that day.
He gave man an image and form to be like Him and free from harm
He took the dust and molded his thoughts.
He gave man an image and form.
He breathed His breath into man.
Only then could man take a stand.
The man was made whole and became a living soul.
We came into time and now to renew our mind
We find who we are in time.
We find purpose in time.
We find what is important in time.
Time helps us develop what we were created for
Time will lead us to heaven's open door where God
builds and restores
As His love surrounds us more and more.

Understanding

Say grasshopper, what's the word for today
I spoke to my Master and He showed me the way.
First, He said attend to my understanding
And knowledge of the Holy Spirit is understanding.
Well, put those words right under your hat so
You can meditate on that.
Attending to the Word is where it is at.
So, to attend to the Word of God we must do our part
As we look to God and obey His way we will not stray
In **Proverbs 2:10-11**
It clearly states: "When Wisdom enters into thine heart and knowledge is pleasant unto the soul, discretion shall preserve thee, understanding shall keep thee."
Understand God, He relates to your heart.
Understand man and the purpose of God's plan.
Understand why man was created in the image of God.
Understand our position in the plan to redeem man.
Understanding is the key to God's way.

Victory

The grasshopper and I were at war again
By now he should know I'll win because
Jesus and I are friends.
In **John 5:4**
"Whatsoever is born of God overcometh the world
And this is the victory that overcame the world, even our faith."
That victory is in all God's children
They must be taught the scripture.
Thine O Lord, is the greatest, the power, the glory,
the victory, and majesty.
Psalm 98:1: "Oh sing unto the Lord a new song for He has done
Marvelous things. His right hand and his holy arm
Hath gotten him the victory."
There is a VICTORY walk in JESUS!
There is a VICTORY talk in JESUS!
There is a VICTORY way in JESUS!
There is a VICTORY song in JESUS!
The children of the Most High God know there is
VICTORY in Him!
Now to end up not in defeat, you must learn at Jesus' feet.
Take His Word and let that be your meat.
Fill your heart, so you can do your part.
With His Word in your heart.
The Word of God is your spiritual meat
Say it; digest it into your heart.
Do your part, and trust the Living God.

Workmanship

Well grasshopper, what's new today
I guess you thought you should have your way
Let's look at what Jesus had to say
Looking into the Book of Life
I came upon some startling advice.
You see, Jesus was the plan of God
To work with men and convert the heart.
Ephesians 2:10 says:
"We are His workmanship created in Christ Jesus unto good works which God hath before ordained that we should walk in them."
John 3:5 says:
"Except a man be born of water and the Spirit he cannot enter into the kingdom of God."
Now read that slow and the truth of God will show
Jesus was the example you know.
Watching Him will let you know what direction to go
For your good works to show.

Your Heart

Oh Grasshopper, have I got a clue for you.
It is about the Lord and it is true!
The fear of the Lord is the beginning of wisdom.
Fear of the Lord means to reverence Him
To have respect for Him and love Him from a pure and clean heart.
Did you know only the purest of hearts shall see God?
The books of Proverbs tells us to guard our heart for out it
Come the issues of life.
The issues of life are to stay out of strife.
Grasshopper, you have done your job well
To get man to believe the lies you tell
And let them send them straight to hell.
Jesus said in **Mark 10:39**
"He that findeth his life shall lose it;
And he that loseth his life for my sake shall find it."
Oh Grasshopper, the heart is the spirit of man that
Has been redeemed by God's own hand.
It is the candle for God to make a pure heart
Your lies deceive man, but the truth of God will help him stand in
this land.

Annie L. Varner

Looking at the Cross

ON THE CROSS HE HUNG AND DIED
The blood rushed from His side
TO SAVE ALL MANKIND.
IT was the perfect SACRIFICE FOR YOU AND ME
The blood that never loses its power
It flows into my mind the benefit for all mankind.
The blood flows into my heart conquering and
restoring me for my part
Now grasshopper, you can hang your head, because you
are a defeated foe
For the grace of God now flows, Jesus did it all so man
could stand tall
Now move out of our way, your deeds will not make us stray
Because GOD has the final say and the blood washed our sins away.

Deliverance

The Grasshopper stood looking at me and I said, "Deliverance has
set me free!"
I am free to move in the land and take a stand
A stand on dominion over the works of God's hand.
He gave me the right at the beginning of time, so that
right is all mine.
Now, turn around and go your way for your rebellion you must pay.
Man now has a chance to celebrate and to accept his new date
When you started out to deceive you started out with Adam and Eve
You got them on your side for a time and space
To destroy the human race.
As soon as God stepped in, your work and plan came to an end
He sat man back on his course to be delivered and set free
and to live in liberty.
Salvation is a mighty work, not looking back at the past.

Annie L. Varner

Being Free

As the wind blew across my face
I thought about the human race.
Jesus appeared in my mind
True life can I find?
Being baptized and allowing the Holy Spirit to live in me.
The Holy Spirit was the link
To God that made me think.
I must renew my mind before I run out of time.
Walking along the dusty road
The beauty of nature began to unfold.
I saw the sunshine bright and pictured the starts at night.
In the gentle breeze, I saw the moving trees.
Then, as my eyes turned toward the fence
I saw the grasshopper looking at me
But I just laughed and laughed and said,
"I am free! I am free! Because of what Jesus did for me!
I am free living in liberty!"
As I looked on, I saw the animals running free
Because of Jesus' life, death, and resurrection
Now, I am set free to be what God wants me to be.

The Table

The table was set and dinner was served
It was then the voices were heard.
What is the purpose of this world?
I heard the voice say, "Jesus will be the way."
Looking at the crossroad of time
Let us keep Jesus in mind.
He came to this earth for a short stay
To remind us of the Master's way.
Purpose was what brought Him here
Stand in awe and do not fear.
The plan came straight from God's hand
It is about deliverance for man.
Before the foundation of the world
Man was preordained by God
With a message from his heart.
You have a purpose for eternity
A purpose to be a part of me.
You have a place to start and that is in your heart.
You have to take a step at a time until you renew your mind.
Take the seed of what you know and let it grow.

Mark 4:13

"Jesus said unto them, know ye not this parable? And how then
Will you know all parables?
The sower, soweth the word."

As you sow the WORD of God, it will take root in your heart.

Purpose

Man was preordained by God with a message from His heart
Man has a purpose for eternity
A purpose to be a part of Me.
Take your cup in your hand and face life with a firm stand
You were chosen to fulfill your purpose
You alone hold that key and that is why you are special to meme.

Psalm 139:16 (GNV)

"God you saw me before I was born, the days allotted to me, had all been recorded
In Your book, before any of them ever began."
Purpose was the plan to be carried out by man
As we start out each day a new, show us what to do.
Give us grace to stay in your race.
Taking purpose in our hand standing firm in the land
Taking purpose in our mind, working with time.
Taking purpose in our soul, allowing You God to make the mold to make us whole.

- **P** for the Praise I give to You
- **U** for Understanding
- **R** for Your Righteousness
- **P** for Purpose to claim I belong to You Lord
- **O** for You Ordained me
- **S** for Salvation
- **E** for Eternity, we will reign with You Lord

Do You Know Him?

Man must know the way to God is not a show
Jesus is the greatest power I know.
He was meek and lowly in heart
He was the Son of God doing His part.
His mind was set for the Master's plan to be met.
To know Him is to Love Him
To know Him is to understand the reason for man
To know Him is the relationship He planned for your part
to restore man.
He sent Jesus: The Way, The Truth and The Light; follow Him
with all your might.
Jesus left His Heavenly home for purpose and time to
help all mankind.
To know God is to understand, your purpose is His command, for
God holds your life in His Hand.
He is King of all Kings. He is the Ruler of all rules.
He is the Greatest of all Greatness; He alone is Holy.
God is to be worshipped and adored
Praised and given glory and honor and power for He created all
And wants to restore us back from the fall.

Searching

I've searched the lands to find the pot of gold
But I know it is only in peace in my soul.
I want to process the rainbow in my heart,
Making decision on my part.
Each color is significant to my spirit
For to find that from within, only then can you win.

I've searched the land to find God
But I know that He is everywhere, in a smile, in a dream, in all truth, in all kindness, in all mankind, in understanding, in true belief, in the air, in the river, in the stars.
Why? Because the entire universe is God.
Search no more for God lives in your heart
Waiting for you to do your part, His life in you will show as you pass through His door.
The door of eternal bliss for with God you cannot miss.
He is the Almighty One that gives love not harm
Now look beyond for what God has already done, through
His only begotten Son.

Your Temple

You are the temple of God; He dwells in your heart
Now you have to do your part.
Keep it clean by dwelling on His Word.
Keep your body undefiled; keep your mind out of worldly mess.
The mind is a valuable possession; be very sure it's anchored on the Solid Rock
That rock is Jesus!
Begin to talk to God, so you can pass the test.
God will hear your call and help you stand tall.
You are
a new creature, just renew your mind.
Forgetting those things which are behind.

About the Author

Rev. Annie L. Varner was born in Opelika, Alabama. At a very early age, she accepted Jesus Christ as her personal Lord and Savior. She knew it was her duty to follow the will of God. Reverend Varner understood that those whom God calls must be grounded in His Holy Word, and they should develop their skills in Christian discipleship before they answer the call to ministry.

Reverend Varner's first step in answering God's call was to join a "working church" where the foundation of God's Word would be placed in her heart. She completed a two-year course of study in Christian Counseling at the Halpine Church School. To develop a sound ministry foundation, she enrolled at the Metropolitan Faith Center School of Ministry. She completed a two-year program that included courses in: The Gifts of the Holy Spirit, Faith, Christian Counseling, Healing Truth, Church, the Life and Ministry of Jesus, Praise and Worship, Pastoral Excellence and Education, Sermon Preparation, and the Ministry of Family.

In 1994, Reverend Varner joined the Church of St. Martin de Porres. This allowed her the opportunity to put her beliefs into action. She headed many ministries from feeding the homeless to leading Bible study. She used every opportunity to share the love and Gospel of Jesus Christ. She also sponsored quarterly prayer breakfasts and assisted the pastor with baptisms and dedications.

In 1999, she began training for the Deaconate and in 2004; she was elevated to the position of Reverend. She summarizes her life experiences as, "The call that was always there," firmly believing the New Testament is clear concerning God's call on the life of all believers. As believers, we are to assume a new identity. God sees us as joint heirs with His Son Jesus. We are His Ambassadors commissioned to take the message of the Gospel throughout the world.

While serving at Doctor's Hospital in Lanham Maryland as a Chaplain, she was inspired to write "The Mind of a Grasshopper." She has always believed it to be her Christian duty to guide others to have the mind of Christ and to always see themselves as more than how they see themselves.

In 2010, feeling a call from God to witness to young people, she formed her program called "On His Wings of Eagles." She holds this event bi-annually. This program was designed to give youth a platform to showcase their skills and talents, as well as to nourish them spiritually.

In 2014, she graduated from Greater Mount Calvary Bible Institute with a certificate in Ministry.

Reverend Varner continues to spread the Gospel and is working on a several projects that will encourage others in the Word of God.

Made in the USA
Middletown, DE
24 November 2017